APOSTLES

BUILDERS, FATHERS, AND ARCHITECTS OF THE KINGDOM

TOM CORNELL

SOZO PUBLISHING

CONTENTS

INTRODUCTION
REDISCOVERING THE ROLE OF THE APOSTLE

We are living in a time of divine reformation. God is restoring what has been lost, neglected, or misunderstood in His Church. Among the most vital restorations in this hour is the return of true apostolic leadership — not in title only, but in function, fruit, and spiritual authority. What was once relegated to history or misunderstood as a missionary office is now being clarified, revealed, and re-established by the Spirit of God.

The word apostle has been stretched, confused, and even abused in modern Christian circles. For some, it's a badge of honor to be worn; for others, it's a mysterious or controversial idea that feels disconnected from local church life. Yet the early Church was built on the foundation of the apostles and prophets, with Christ Jesus as the cornerstone (Ephesians 2:20). That foundation was not temporary. It was never meant to be replaced with organizational management or celebrity Christianity. It was designed to remain — continuing to shape how the Church is governed, how the Kingdom is expanded, and how sons and daughters are raised into maturity.

This book is not about elevating one office over another. Every gift in the fivefold ministry matters, and all are essential for equipping the saints and building up the Body of Christ. But we must understand: apostles are not simply pastors with extra ambition. They are not entrepreneurs with spiritual language. Nor are they missionaries with a business card. Apostles are sent ones, commissioned by Christ, to govern, build, and multiply the Kingdom. They are foundation-layers, culture-setters, movement-starters, and spiritual architects. They don't just lead churches — they build apostolic ecosystems that shape generations.

In many places, the Church has inherited a pastoral model that emphasizes care, comfort, and maintenance. While those elements are needed, they are insufficient to fulfill the global mandate of the Great Commission. Apostles bring government where there is chaos, clarity where there is confusion, and expansion where there has been stagnation. Their very presence signals movement, order, and alignment. True apostles carry blueprints from Heaven and the burden to build according to the mind of Christ. They don't seek to be followed — they seek to reproduce. They don't gather for power — they gather to send.

But to truly honor and partner with apostolic grace, we must first understand what apostles do. This book is a Kingdom invitation to rediscover the function and fruit of apostleship — not as a theory, but as a living reality. Whether you are an emerging apostolic leader, part of an apostolic house, or simply hungry to understand what God is restoring in this generation, this book is for you.

We will explore the core roles of apostles — from establishing Kingdom government and spiritual fathering, to equipping fivefold teams and confronting doctrinal error. We will see how apostles create systems for multiplication, carry supernatural authority, and unify the Body of Christ for Kingdom advancement. Each chapter will not only teach but activate — calling you to align with apostolic grace in your own life, ministry, or calling.

In a world of shallow titles and superficial platforms, God is raising up builders again. True apostles who will not flinch at the cost, compromise for applause, or build without a blueprint. This book is dedicated to those who feel the weight of the Kingdom and the ache for God's government to be made manifest on earth as it is in Heaven. It's time to rediscover what apostles do — and to respond with reverence, alignment, and faith.

1

APOSTLES ARE SENT ONES — REDISCOVERING APOSTOLIC IDENTITY

I f you strip away the modern assumptions and titles, the word apostle simply means "sent one." Derived from the Greek word apostolos, it speaks of someone who is commissioned with authority, sent on assignment, and expected to represent the sender fully. In the ancient world, an apostolos was more than a messenger — they were an envoy empowered to act on behalf of the kingdom or empire they represented. This was not a symbolic role. It carried legal weight, governmental authority, and cultural responsibility.

When Jesus chose twelve men and named them apostles (Luke 6:13), He was not assigning a religious title. He was giving them a Kingdom identity and a governmental function. They were called to represent Him — not just with words, but with authority, power, and alignment to Heaven. That calling did not expire with the Twelve. Ephesians 4:11-13 makes it clear: apostles, prophets, evangelists, pastors, and teachers were given to the Church until we all reach unity, maturity, and fullness in Christ. That work is ongoing — and so is the need for true apostles.

Sent by God, Not Self-Appointed

Apostles are not self-made. They are called, formed, tested, and sent by God. The apostle Paul made this clear over and over again. He opened his letters by stating, "Paul, an apostle of Christ Jesus by the will of God" (Ephesians 1:1 ESV). He did not take the title as a personal ambition. He received the call through divine encounter and was confirmed through fruit, authority, and suffering.

In today's context, many people claim apostolic status due to success, influence, or visibility. But the true mark of an apostle is not how many people follow them — it is how clearly they follow the voice of the One who sent them. Apostles are not promoted by popularity. They are proven by their obedience to divine commission.

Apostles Carry Assignment, Not Just Anointing

One of the great misunderstandings in the Church today is confusing anointing with assignment. A person may have a powerful gift — healing, prophecy, preaching — and yet not be called as an apostle. Apostles don't just move in power; they move with specific direction from the throne of God. They are builders, not just blessers. They carry blueprints, not just burdens.

Apostolic identity is rooted in the weight of divine responsibility. Apostles are not merely called to attend church — they are sent to establish and govern it. They are not just people who "go"; they are people who are sent with a mandate to advance the rule of Christ and establish spiritual government where there has been none.

Apostles Walk in Identity Before They Walk in Office

Before Jesus officially commissioned His apostles, He spent time forming their identity. They walked with Him, learned from Him, were corrected by Him, and grew in love for Him. Apostleship is not earned through performance. It is cultivated through proximity and transformation. The true apostle is not merely skilled; they are surrendered.

This is why apostolic identity must be grounded in sonship. An apostle is first and foremost a son of God who walks in intimacy, obedience, and submission. From that place of sonship, they carry authority. When identity is not secure, authority becomes manipulation. But when identity is rooted in sonship, authority flows in humility, sacrifice, and grace.

Apostles Represent Heaven, Not Themselves

A true apostle lives to represent the culture, character, and command of Heaven. Just as a Roman apostolos was sent to a newly conquered territory to teach Roman customs and implement Roman systems, so Kingdom apostles are sent to shape culture, not accommodate it. They are ambassadors of another world, transforming environments to reflect the King they represent.

This means apostles must walk in both revelation and representation. They must know what Heaven is saying, and they must demonstrate what Heaven looks like. Their lives become a message — a living epistle — that speaks of the Kingdom. Apostles are not culture chameleons. They are culture shapers, sent to bring order, truth, and transformation.

Apostles Embrace Sacrifice for the Sake of the Assignment

The apostolic call is costly. Paul described himself as a man who was "hard pressed on every side... struck down, but not destroyed" (2 Corinthians 4:8-9 NIV). He bore the marks of Jesus in his body and carried the burden of the churches in his heart. Apostles do not seek comfort — they embrace the cross.

Modern church culture often glamorizes leadership, but apostleship is marked by suffering, sacrifice, and spiritual warfare. Apostles carry weight in the spirit. They intercede, they weep, they contend. Their authority comes from dying daily, not from titles or positions. You cannot fake apostolic grace — because the burden will crush anyone who hasn't been called to carry it.

Apostles Move with Heaven's Timing

One of the distinguishing traits of apostolic identity is the ability to move in sync with Heaven's timetable. Apostles do not react to trends — they respond to revelation. They build when Heaven says build, they send when Heaven says send, and they wait when Heaven says wait. Their authority flows from alignment, not activity. Because they are sent ones, apostles understand that the timing of their actions matters just as much as the actions themselves. Like Jesus, who said, "I only do what I see my Father doing"* (John 5:19), apostles are governed by divine timing. They are tuned to the voice of the Spirit and are unafraid to be early, late, or out of sync with man's opinions — as long as they are aligned with Heaven.

Apostles Birth Movements, Not Just Ministries

At their core, apostles are movement carriers. While pastors

---

* Paraphrase

tend to gather and prophets tend to call out, apostles build ecosystems. They create environments where sons and daughters can grow, gifts can be activated, and cultures can be transformed. Apostles think generationally. They are always asking, "How can we multiply this? How can we leave a legacy?"

This is why apostolic identity cannot be reduced to planting a church or starting a ministry. Apostles are not called to build monuments — they are called to launch movements that continue long after they are gone. Their fruit is not in what they personally lead, but in what they multiply through others.

Reflection Questions:

1. Have I mistaken the apostolic for something institutional or formal rather than relational and missional?
2. Am I building something I was sent to build — or something I decided to build?
3. Do I live from the posture of a son or the pressure of a title?
4. Who am I sent to? What territory, people, or sphere am I called to transform?

Activation Prayer:

Father, I thank You that You are restoring the apostolic in Your Church. I humble myself before You and ask that You reveal to me the areas where I've misunderstood or misrepresented this calling. Teach me what it means to be sent by You — not for ambition or platform, but for the fulfillment of Your purposes. Anchor me in sonship, align me with Your timing, and give me the grace to carry what You've entrusted to me. Let my life be marked by obedience, humility, and movement. In Jesus' name, amen.

2

GOVERNING WITH KINGDOM AUTHORITY

"This is why I left you in Crete, so that you might put what remained into order, and appoint elders in every town as I directed you" (Titus 1:5 ESV)

When Paul wrote this to Titus, he wasn't sending a friend to oversee a casual ministry project. He was delegating apostolic authority to establish Kingdom government. Apostles don't just inspire movements — they govern them. They bring Heaven's alignment into earthly chaos. They set in order what is out of order, not by force, but by spiritual authority rooted in obedience to Christ.

Unfortunately, in much of the modern Church, the idea of governance has been misunderstood. For some, it has been abused — creating hierarchies of control or manipulation. For others, it's been avoided — leaving churches with no real order, no accountability, and no enduring fruit. But when properly understood, apostolic government is not about control; it's about Kingdom alignment. It is about Heaven's structure manifesting on earth, so the Church can function in power, purity, and purpose.

Authority That Comes from Heaven

Apostolic authority doesn't originate from man. It is not conferred through degrees, denominations, or organizational promotions. It is given by Christ Himself, evidenced through spiritual fruit, recognized by other mature leaders, and demonstrated in the ability to govern well. Jesus said,

> "All authority in heaven and on earth has been given to me. Go therefore..." (Matthew 28:18–19 ESV).

Apostles operate under that authority. They do not walk in presumption; they walk in delegated authority. That authority is tested, refined, and matured over time, as apostles learn to govern not just people but their own spirit, family, and ministry life. When apostolic government is rightly embraced, it brings freedom, not bondage; clarity, not confusion; multiplication, not micromanagement. True authority brings life.

Bringing Order Where There Has Been Chaos

One of the clearest signs of apostolic grace is the ability to bring divine order. The Greek word taxis, often translated as "order," speaks of arrangement, alignment, and proper placement. Where there is apostolic authority, things that have been misaligned begin to shift into place.

Paul left Titus in Crete because the churches were functioning without structure. Elders had not been appointed. The churches lacked unified culture and vision. Paul's solution was not to entertain them or merely preach to them — it was to govern them. This required identifying leaders, setting standards, establishing doctrine, and aligning the church with Heaven's pattern.

Apostolic order doesn't crush creativity. It creates the framework in which creativity can flourish. Like bones in a body, governance provides the structure that enables movement and growth. Without it, churches devolve into chaos or drift aimlessly with no lasting impact.

Apostles Build Government, Not Just Gatherings

The apostolic call is not simply to preach inspiring sermons or gather large crowds. Apostles are builders — not just of physical places, but of spiritual government and structure. Paul described himself as a "wise master builder" (1 Corinthians 3:10), laying foundations on which others could build. This kind of building is intentional, strategic, and spiritual in nature.

Apostles establish the culture, doctrine, leadership structure, and accountability systems necessary for the Church to function as a Kingdom embassy on earth. This includes:

- Appointing elders who reflect maturity, character, and faith
- Creating relational alignment between leaders and teams
- Setting doctrinal boundaries that protect truth
- Delegating responsibility to trusted leaders who carry the house DNA

Apostolic governance is about equipping others to function within God's order so that the Church grows in unity, strength, and multiplication.

Kingdom Government vs. Religious Control

There's a vast difference between Kingdom government and religious control. Kingdom government is always rooted in honor, alignment, and empowerment. It doesn't seek to control people's decisions — it seeks to position them for maximum impact and maturity. Apostolic government respects the freedom of individuals while protecting the integrity of the whole.

In contrast, religious control manipulates people to maintain power or protect insecurities. It creates systems that elevate a leader but disempower the body. It fosters fear, not faith — and dependency, not discipleship. True apostles do not use people to build their ministries. They build people to fulfill their callings. They govern with a towel in one hand and authority in the other — serving while leading, correcting while covering, releasing while aligning.

The Apostolic Grace to Appoint and Align Leaders

In Acts 14:23, Paul and Barnabas,

"appointed elders for them in every church, with prayer and fasting."
ESV

Apostles don't merely suggest leaders — they appoint them. This isn't done by popularity or democratic vote; it is a spiritual discernment process, often confirmed by prophetic witness and the fruit of maturity. Appointing leaders is one of the most sacred responsibilities in apostolic governance. It sets the trajectory of the house for years to come.

True apostles discern character, alignment, and capacity,

not just charisma or availability. But appointing leaders isn't enough — apostles also work to align them. Alignment means that leaders don't just carry responsibility; they carry the heart and vision of the apostolic house. They function in unity of spirit, not just in task execution. Alignment is what enables government to multiply healthily, without division or distortion.

Apostolic Government Brings Protection and Power

Many believers resist the idea of governance because they've been hurt by abusive leaders or controlling systems. But the absence of government doesn't create safety — it creates vulnerability. Apostolic government provides covering, clarity, and protection. When apostolic order is established:

- Wolves are exposed, and sheep are protected
- Doctrinal confusion is addressed, and sound teaching is restored
- Dysfunction is corrected, and healing is administered
- Vision becomes clear, and mission becomes sustainable

A church or ministry without apostolic government may seem free for a season, but eventually it will lack the power to endure and multiply. Apostles don't just protect the house — they position it for sustained growth and spiritual power.

Government That Releases, Not Restricts

True apostles govern to release people, not to restrict them. Their authority does not suppress growth — it unlocks it. Under apostolic alignment, people discover their callings, are equipped for ministry, and are sent with clarity and covering.

Apostles understand that government is not about control — it's about flow. Just as arteries and veins create structure for blood to flow through the body, apostolic government creates channels for the Spirit to flow through the Church. Without structure, there is spillage and loss. With Kingdom government, there is flow and fruitfulness.

Reflection Questions:

1. Do I view spiritual government as something restrictive or life-giving?
2. Am I aligned under apostolic leadership that brings order and clarity?
3. How do I respond when correction or alignment is required in my life?
4. Is the ministry or organization I serve in structured for control or for release?

Activation Prayer:

Father, thank You for Your wisdom in establishing government in Your Kingdom. I repent for the times I've misunderstood or resisted Your divine order. Teach me to value alignment, accountability, and authority as gifts that protect and release me. I ask for discernment to recognize true apostolic government — and the humility to come into proper alignment. Raise up builders in this generation who will lead not with control, but with compassion and courage. In Jesus' name, amen.

3

BUILDING WHAT
HEAVEN HAS REVEALED

When Paul called himself a "wise master builder" in 1 Corinthians 3:10, he was describing the essential apostolic function of building what Heaven has revealed. Apostles are not just preachers or organizers — they are spiritual architects, entrusted with blueprints from God and anointing to construct what aligns with Heaven's design. Their assignment is not to replicate religious trends or imitate popular models, but to receive divine instruction and implement it with precision, patience, and power.

True apostolic building begins with revelation, not replication. God never asked His apostles to build according to man's ideas. He gave them heavenly strategies, divine patterns, and prophetic insight. Apostles are called to build according to what they see in the Spirit, not what they admire in the flesh. The result is a structure that carries the weight of glory, the authority of Heaven, and the capacity to reproduce sons and daughters in the Kingdom.

The Apostle as a Wise Master Builder

In 1 Corinthians 3:10, Paul writes:

"According to the grace of God given to me, like a skilled master builder I laid a foundation, and someone else is building upon it." ESV

The word "master builder" comes from the Greek architekton — the origin of our English word "architect." It speaks of someone who not only builds but designs, plans, and oversees construction. Apostles are not just involved in ministry; they are responsible for the design and health of the entire structure. They build with eternity in mind.

This building grace comes from God. Paul said it was "according to the grace given to me." Apostles don't choose this role — they're given grace and blueprints to fulfill it. That grace enables them to:

- See the big picture
- Discern timing
- Establish foundations
- Correct faulty structures
- Build for generational impact

Where pastors often tend to the flock and teachers build line upon line, apostles construct environments that reflect the culture, government, and values of the Kingdom.

Building from Revelation, Not Replication

Apostolic builders must resist the temptation to copy others. While wisdom can be gleaned from leaders and models, apostolic ministry requires direct revelation from Heaven. Moses was warned on Mount Sinai:

"Be sure that you make everything according to the pattern I have shown you here on the mountain" (Exodus 25:40 NLT)

That pattern was sacred. Moses didn't have the liberty to add or remove details. He was a builder under instruction. Likewise, apostles today must receive from God before they build for God. Revelation precedes implementation.

This means apostles are often ahead of their time. They build things people don't fully understand yet — training centers, apostolic houses, family-based discipleship structures, or economic models that break poverty cycles. But if the pattern is from Heaven, the fruit will come. Revelation is always the seed of reformation.

Apostolic Blueprints Carry Generational Impact

Apostles do not build for the moment — they build for movement. Their structures are designed not just to meet today's need, but to shape future generations. This is why Paul was so focused on foundation. He understood that the quality of the foundation determines the future of the house. Apostles lay foundations by:

- Establishing Kingdom doctrine
- Cultivating honor and spiritual alignment
- Defining mission and values
- Building relational and governmental systems

These foundations outlive the apostle and create momentum for sons and daughters to rise. The true test of apostolic building is not the size of the crowd, but the stability of the culture and the fruit that endures beyond the builder's presence.

Apostolic Building Requires War and Work

Every true builder must carry both a sword and a trowel (see Nehemiah 4:17). Apostles are called to build while they battle — facing opposition from religious spirits, demonic assignments, and even misunderstanding within the Church. Apostles must:

- War in prayer to break resistance over regions
- Contend against compromise, idolatry, and cultural confusion
- Navigate betrayal, delay, and false accusation
- Maintain courage and clarity when others doubt the process

Building requires more than revelation. It demands resolve. Apostles build under pressure, not for applause, and their eyes remain fixed on the pattern of Heaven — even when the ground beneath them is shaking.

The Difference Between Ministry and Movement

Ministry focuses on people. Movements focus on people who will multiply. Apostles do not simply create a ministry platform — they birth apostolic ecosystems where leaders are raised, sons are sent, and new territory is taken. They think in terms of systems, structures, and legacy.

While a pastor may ask:

"How are the people doing?"

An apostle asks:

"Is the culture replicating? Is the foundation reproducing? Is the Kingdom expanding?"

Apostolic builders don't just ask:

"How do we gather more people?" but "How do we build people who carry the DNA of this house into other regions, cities, and spheres?"

This movement mindset causes apostles to equip, empower, and release rather than retain.

The Danger of Building Without Blueprint

Many churches and ministries are busy building — but not all are building with Heaven's design. Some are building for success, applause, or survival. But any structure not founded on the Word, presence, and government of God will eventually collapse. Jesus warned in Matthew 7 about those who build on sand versus those who build on rock. Apostles are obsessed with foundations because they know storms will come. If the structure is built to impress but not to endure, it will not last. True apostolic ministry constantly asks:

- Did God tell me to build this?
- Am I building according to the pattern, or public pressure?
- Is Christ truly the cornerstone of what I'm constructing?

These questions protect the builder's heart and ensure the house reflects the King.

Apostles Build People, Not Just Places

Perhaps the most important truth: apostles are called to build people. The apostolic mandate is not fulfilled in buildings or logos — it is fulfilled in sons and daughters who walk in truth, power, and maturity. Paul's heart was not consumed with structures, but with people formed in Christ.

"My little children, for whom I am again in the anguish of childbirth until Christ is formed in you!" (Galatians 4:19 ESV)

Apostles labor until Christ is formed — not just in individuals, but in communities, teams, and generations. Buildings may fade. Platforms may change. But the people apostles build will carry Kingdom legacy into every sphere of society — family, business, government, education, and beyond.

Reflection Questions:

1. Am I building from revelation or imitation?
2. Has God given me a blueprint for what I am called to build?
3. Am I building for the crowd or for Kingdom culture?
4. What kind of legacy will my structure leave behind?

Activation Prayer:

Father, I ask for Your wisdom to build according to Your pattern. I surrender every man-made idea, trend-driven plan, or self-driven ambition. Give me eyes to see what You are building and ears to hear the instructions of Heaven. Let me not just build places but build people — sons and daughters who carry Your Kingdom everywhere they go. Strengthen me to battle while building and to endure in faith when the process is hard. I declare: I will build what Heaven has revealed. In Jesus' name, amen.

4

ADVANCING INTO NEW TERRITORY

Apostles are not maintainers of the status quo — they are pioneers of new territory. The apostolic grace is inherently forward-moving, trailblazing, and expansion-driven. Where some are called to steward what has been built, apostles are called to advance the Kingdom into new places, new people groups, and even new sectors of society. They are Heaven's "sent ones," deployed into spiritual darkness to establish light, order, and influence. Paul described his apostolic ambition this way:

"It has always been my ambition to preach the gospel where Christ was not known, so that I would not be building on someone else's foundation" (Romans 15:20 NIV)

This statement reveals the heart of every true apostle: territorial advancement. Apostles carry a grace to break ground, to take regions, and to establish Christ's Lordship where it has not yet been seen. Whether that territory is geographical, cultural, or generational, apostles move with the authority of the One who sends them — to uproot, plant, build, and multiply.

Apostles Carry a Territorial Mandate

Unlike other fivefold leaders who focus primarily on people, apostles often see regions and systems. While pastors shepherd individuals and teachers explain truth, apostles ask questions like:

- What territory is unreached?
- What systems need to be reformed?
- What cities or nations are under demonic influence?
- How do we shift the spiritual atmosphere over this place?

This territorial lens is not about ego or empire. It's about assignment and authority. Just as Jesus said, "I must preach the good news of the kingdom of God to the other towns also, because that is why I was sent"* (Luke 4:43), so apostles live with a sent urgency to go where others won't and to pioneer what others haven't. They may be called to take new neighborhoods, cities, campuses, or even whole industries — media, government, education, or business. Apostolic grace transcends church walls and empowers Kingdom expansion in every sphere.

Breaking Ground Requires Apostolic Courage

Advancing into new territory isn't glamorous. It's gritty. Every new territory is guarded by old giants. Just like Israel faced resistance in Canaan, apostles encounter opposition, warfare, and systems of intimidation when taking ground. Apostles are called to:

---

* NIV

- Confront entrenched religious structures
- Tear down principalities ruling over regions
- Persevere when there's little fruit at first
- Model faith in hostile or barren environments

This kind of ground-breaking requires apostolic courage — the ability to obey God in the face of fear, to keep building in the face of resistance, and to move forward when others retreat. True apostles are not easily discouraged. They are fueled by revelation and vision, not public applause.

Apostles See Potential Where Others See Problems

One of the distinguishing marks of apostolic grace is prophetic sight for territory. Apostles can look at a broken city, a failing church, or a forgotten people group and see potential, not just pain. Like Nehemiah surveying the ruins of Jerusalem, apostles see what can be when others only see what's wrong. This ability to see potential leads apostles to:

- Plant churches in overlooked neighborhoods
- Invest in young leaders others would pass over
- Launch movements in dry places
- Rebuild where others have abandoned

Apostles don't just inherit ground — they reclaim and redeem it. They carry the heart of Heaven for regions and rise up as gatekeepers and reformers, willing to labor for the sake of legacy.

The Spirit of Religion Resists Apostolic Advancement

Wherever apostles go, the spirit of religion often rises to meet them. The religious spirit values control over transformation, form over power, and tradition over truth. When apostles begin to advance into new territory, that spirit reacts — often through criticism, accusation, or opposition from other leaders. Just like Paul was repeatedly challenged by Judaizers and false apostles, today's apostolic leaders must discern and overcome religious resistance. This includes:

- Opposition from those threatened by change
- Accusations of pride or rebellion
- Misunderstanding from people stuck in old wineskins
- Warfare that tries to isolate, distract, or discredit them

But where religion resists, the Kingdom prevails. Apostles are graced to keep moving forward, not to fight people but to overturn systems that keep regions in bondage.

Apostolic Advancement Is Backed by Supernatural Power

Territorial advancement requires more than vision — it requires power. Wherever apostles go, they carry the authority to demonstrate the Kingdom through miracles, deliverance, healing, and prophetic demonstration. Paul wrote:

"I fully proclaimed the gospel of Christ by the power of signs and wonders, through the power of the Spirit of God. So from Jerusalem all the way around to Illyricum, I have fully proclaimed the gospel of Christ" (Romans 15:19 NIV)

That means Kingdom advancement isn't just about preaching — it's about demonstrating the superiority of Christ's Kingdom over every other power. Apostles move in power to:

- Break strongholds over people and places
- Confirm the message of the Kingdom
- Reveal the reality of Jesus as King

Without power, new territory remains resistant. But when the Kingdom comes in word and power, hearts open, regions shift, and the gates of Hell cannot prevail.

Advancing the Kingdom in Every Sphere of Society

Apostolic advancement is not limited to church planting. Apostles today are being sent into business, politics, education, media, and beyond. These cultural "mountains" are territories that influence how people think, believe, and behave. When apostles are sent into these spaces, they bring:

- Kingdom strategy to reform systems
- Spiritual authority to displace darkness
- Relational grace to build teams and ecosystems
- Prophetic insight to see and shape the future

For example:

- An apostle in government may draft legislation shaped by righteousness.
- An apostle in business may create wealth structures that fund Kingdom missions.
- An apostle in media may birth platforms that release truth and tear down lies.

These apostles may not be on a stage or behind a pulpit — but they are advancing the Kingdom just as powerfully.

Apostles Leave Tracks for Others to Follow

Apostles don't just take territory — they create pathways for others. Once a new area is broken open, they equip and release teams to multiply the work. Apostles never think in terms of personal achievement. They think in terms of movement multiplication. Their goal is not to be the only one advancing, but to:

- Equip pioneers
- Commission sons and daughters
- Raise local leaders
- Hand over territory to those who will steward it well

Apostolic advancement is always unto reproduction. Apostles don't just open doors — they raise up gatekeepers who can hold the ground, build the house, and expand the vision.

Reflection Questions:

1. What new territory has God placed in front of me that I have resisted or overlooked?
2. Am I willing to pioneer where no one else has gone — even if it's hard?
3. Do I see potential in people and places others have forgotten?
4. Am I building a life and ministry that multiplies and creates space for others?

Activation Prayer:

Father, I thank You that You are always advancing. You do not retreat or fear resistance. I ask that You place within me the apostolic courage to go where You send me, to see what You see, and to build what You've revealed. I break agreement with fear, passivity, and comfort. I receive grace to take new territory — not in my strength, but in Your authority. Use my life to shift regions, displace darkness, and establish Your Kingdom. In Jesus' name, amen.

5

EQUIPPING THE FIVEFOLD
AND RAISING TEAMS

O ne of the most important functions of an apostle is not to do all the work of ministry, but to equip others to fulfill their callings. Apostles don't build alone — they build teams, raise leaders, and activate the full fivefold ministry within the Body of Christ. Their fruit is not measured by personal platform but by how many others they have raised, aligned, and released. Ephesians 4:11–12 tells us plainly:

"And He gave some to be apostles, some prophets, some evangelists, and some pastors and teachers, to equip the saints for the work of ministry, for building up the body of Christ..." NKJV

This is not a random list. It is a blueprint for a mature, healthy, and mobilized Church. Apostles are not the only gift, but they are graced to bring alignment to the others. They see the big picture, recognize graces, and ensure that each part of the fivefold is functioning in cooperation — not competition.

When apostles function rightly, they cultivate cultures where everyone is equipped, leaders are raised, and teams carry the vision together. The result is a body that doesn't just attend — it advances.

Apostles Equip the Saints, Not Entertain the Crowd

The word "equip" in Ephesians 4 comes from the Greek katartismos, which means to mend, restore, or prepare for full function. Apostolic ministry isn't about entertaining or spoon-feeding believers — it's about restoring people to wholeness and activating them for Kingdom purpose.

Apostles understand that the Church is not an audience to impress, but an army to deploy. They don't settle for passive churchgoers; they labor to raise:

- Disciples who know how to hear God
- Believers who walk in spiritual authority
- Leaders who multiply and disciple others
- Teams that move in unity and power

The apostolic model is not personality-driven; it's presence-driven and purpose-driven. Apostles don't seek fans — they build families who carry the fire together.

Recognizing and Aligning the Fivefold Gifts

Apostles have a unique grace to recognize the gifts of others. They see beyond behavior and into calling and potential. This means they don't just fill positions — they call people into purpose. Whether it's a hidden teacher, a raw evangelist, or a prophetic voice still developing, apostles are always watching for what God has placed in others. But recognition is not enough. Apostles also bring alignment. They help each fivefold gift:

- Understand their role in the bigger picture
- Function in honor and unity with the other gifts
- Stay within healthy boundaries and character
- Mature into their fullest expression

Without apostolic alignment, the fivefold gifts can operate in silos or tension. The prophet may clash with the pastor. The evangelist may frustrate the teacher. But under apostolic leadership, each gift is valued, guided, and matured. The result is not competition — but collaboration.

Building and Leading Healthy Teams

Apostles are team-builders by nature. They know the Kingdom does not advance through lone rangers but through unified teams who carry shared DNA, shared values, and shared burdens. Apostles model team life, invite others into it, and train their teams to function like families on mission. Healthy apostolic teams are marked by:

- Relational trust — not just task execution
- Clear roles and responsibilities — without rigid control
- Mutual submission and honor — with the apostle leading by example
- Shared revelation and vision — ensuring everyone is pulling in the same direction

Teams under apostolic leadership are not just efficient — they are relationally aligned and spiritually dynamic. They don't merely serve a vision — they become the vision.

Reproducing Sons, Not Just Leaders

True apostles are not content to build with hirelings or transactional leaders. They labor to reproduce sons and daughters — people who carry the heart, spirit, and vision of the house. Paul said to the Corinthians:

"You have many teachers but not many fathers. I became your father through the gospel" (1 Corinthians 4:15 NIV)

This kind of fathering involves:

- Time and intentional investment
- Correction with compassion
- Impartation through relationship, not just information
- Walking through process, not just handing over position

Apostles don't just develop skills; they form identity. They help sons discover who they are in Christ, walk in holiness and wholeness, and mature into leaders who can then raise others. This is how apostolic legacy is built — through relational reproduction, not organizational replication.

Creating Apostolic Cultures of Honor and Empowerment

Every team reflects the culture of its leadership. Apostles who build well create cultures of honor, hunger, and empowerment. In these environments, leaders don't jockey for power or operate in fear. They celebrate one another's grace, correct in love, and serve with joy. An apostolic culture:

- Honors every gift without idolizing any
- Celebrates progress while demanding integrity
- Confronts rebellion and gossip swiftly

- Builds a family, not a factory

In these environments, people are free to grow, safe to fail, and surrounded by others who call them higher. Apostles are responsible for cultivating that atmosphere and protecting it from division, compromise, or carnality.

Apostolic Training Is Ongoing, Not One-Time

Equipping isn't a single class or a conference event. Apostolic equipping is ongoing discipleship — walking with people until they're able to carry the Kingdom for themselves. Jesus didn't just preach to the Twelve — He lived with them, corrected them, empowered them, and then sent them. Likewise, apostles today must commit to walking long-term with those they are equipping. This includes:

- Providing sound doctrine and practical instruction
- Imparting vision and helping others catch the house DNA
- Correcting immaturity or pride when necessary
- Empowering people to take risks, lead others, and multiply

Apostolic equipping trains people for both character and capacity. It's not enough to be gifted — you must be grounded. It's not enough to be passionate — you must be positioned. Apostles ensure both are happening.

The Goal: A Mature, Mobilized Church

Paul's vision for fivefold ministry was clear:

"Until we all attain to the unity of the faith and of the knowledge of

the Son of God, to mature manhood, to the measure of the stature of the fullness of Christ" (Ephesians 4:13 ESV)

The apostle's job is not to keep people dependent — it's to raise them into maturity. To move the Church from passive consumption to active mobilization. To see every saint equipped, every gift activated, and every believer functioning in their God-given calling. When apostles build teams well and equip the fivefold, the result is:

- A unified house
- A mature leadership team
- A multiplied mission
- A church that advances the Kingdom instead of just surviving

Reflection Questions:

1. Who am I equipping, and how am I equipping them?
2. Do I value all fivefold gifts, or have I prioritized one over the others?
3. Is my leadership reproducing sons and daughters or just workers?
4. What kind of team culture am I cultivating — one of honor or one of control?

Activation Prayer:

Father, I thank You for the gifts You've placed in the Body of Christ. I ask for apostolic grace to equip, align, and empower those around me. Teach me to recognize the gold in others, to lead with love and integrity, and to build teams that reflect Your Kingdom. Help me reproduce sons and daughters who carry Your heart, Your vision, and Your holiness. Let my leadership not be about control, but about Christ being fully formed in those I lead. In Jesus' name, amen.

6

SPIRITUAL FATHERING AND APOSTOLIC COVERING

In an age of spiritual orphans, celebrity Christianity, and leaderless churches, one of the greatest needs in the Body of Christ is the restoration of spiritual fathering. Apostles are not merely builders of ministries — they are fathers of movements. They carry the heart of God to cover, correct, protect, and release sons and daughters into their full identity and destiny. Paul makes this distinction clear in 1 Corinthians 4:15:

"Even if you had ten thousand instructors in Christ, you do not have many fathers. For in Christ Jesus I became your father through the gospel." NKJV

Apostles are more than teachers, strategists, or miracle workers. Their primary legacy is not what they build, but who they raise. They take responsibility for people — not just for their gifting, but for their soul, character, and future. Apostolic ministry without fathering becomes sterile, impersonal, and ultimately ineffective. But when fathering is restored, sons arise, houses are established, and legacy is secured.

What Is Spiritual Fathering?

Spiritual fathering is not about age or position — it's about responsibility, relationship, and reproduction. A spiritual father carries the burden to see sons and daughters formed in Christ, walking in maturity, and fulfilling their Kingdom calling. He doesn't use people to build his ministry — he builds people to fulfill their mandate. Spiritual fathering involves:

- Covering — providing safety, support, and spiritual oversight
- Correction — lovingly confronting immaturity, sin, or pride
- Commissioning — recognizing callings and releasing sons into destiny
- Covenant — walking with people through seasons, setbacks, and promotion

Apostles don't create followers. They cultivate sons — those who carry not just the mission, but the DNA of the house.

The Difference Between Teachers and Fathers

Paul contrasts the abundance of instructors with the rarity of fathers. Instructors may pass on knowledge, but fathers pass on identity. Teachers fill your mind — fathers shape your life. Teachers may speak truth, but fathers walk with you in it. The difference can be seen in how they respond to failure:

- A teacher may disqualify you.
- A father will restore you.

In how they give correction:

- A teacher may offer principles.
- A father speaks from love and relationship.

And in how they view your future:

- A teacher prepares you for tests.
- A father prepares you for legacy.

Apostolic fathering is not about owning people, but about owning the responsibility to love, lead, and launch them.

Apostolic Covering: Protection Without Control

Covering is a biblical concept, deeply rooted in God's nature. Throughout Scripture, God is revealed as a covering God — shielding Adam and Eve with skins, covering Israel with a cloud, and covering His people with His wings (Psalm 91:4). Covering represents protection, identity, and spiritual alignment. Apostolic covering functions in the same way:

- It protects leaders and believers from spiritual attack and error.
- It provides accountability and oversight.
- It brings order, safety, and unity in the midst of growth and warfare.

But apostolic covering is not about control. It does not dominate, micromanage, or manipulate. Control is the fruit of insecurity; covering is the fruit of love. True apostles cover so that sons and daughters can rise in strength, not so they stay dependent forever.

Signs of a Healthy Spiritual Covering

Not every claim to covering is healthy. Here are signs that apostolic covering is aligned with Heaven:

- Honor flows both ways — sons honor fathers, and fathers honor sons.
- Correction is given in love, not shame or fear.
- Freedom is encouraged, not suppressed.
- Transparency and trust are cultivated, not forced.
- Covenant is prioritized over convenience.

Covering should never be a trap. It should be a greenhouse for growth, where callings are nurtured and maturity is pursued.

Raising Sons and Daughters in the Kingdom

The greatest legacy of an apostle is not a ministry, building, or brand — it's a generation of sons and daughters walking in maturity and multiplying the mission. Spiritual fathering is about imparting identity and walking with people into destiny. Sons and daughters are not just volunteers — they are:

- Carriers of the house vision
- Protectors of the culture
- Future fathers and mothers in training

Apostles must raise sons who:

- Know how to honor without idolizing
- Serve without striving
- Carry weight without needing a title
- Speak truth without dishonor

When sons are healthy, the movement is healthy. A fatherless movement will eventually fracture. But a fathered movement will multiply.

The Process of Fathering

Spiritual fathering is not instant. It's a process of formation — often messy, slow, and deeply relational. Apostles must be willing to:

- Walk with people in their immaturity
- Confront without wounding
- Encourage even when progress is slow
- Correct in a way that restores, not rejects

Jesus modeled this with His disciples. He didn't just teach them — He lived with them, rebuked them, fed them, sent them, and prayed for them. Apostolic fathering is spiritual parenting, and like parenting, it requires sacrifice, discernment, and endurance.

Covenant Relationships in an Orphan Culture

We live in a world marked by fatherlessness — spiritually and naturally. Many believers carry wounds from absent, abusive, or unavailable fathers. As a result, they enter the Church with orphan mindsets: mistrust, fear of rejection, and a need to perform.

Apostolic fathering confronts this orphan spirit by offering covenant — relationships that don't abandon in hard seasons, that confront lies with truth, and that walk with sons and daughters into healing and wholeness. Covenant relationships:

- Stay through correction

- Forgive offenses
- Seek unity over comfort
- Carry the weight of family, not just function

When apostolic fathers cultivate covenant culture, the orphan spirit is broken, and spiritual families emerge.

Releasing Mature Sons Into Their Own Assignments

Apostolic fathering is not complete until the son is sent. Paul did not hold on to Timothy — he prepared him, affirmed him, and released him. The goal of apostolic covering is not to keep people under your shadow, but to empower them to stand in their own authority. Apostles release sons when:

- Identity is secure
- Character is tested
- Vision is aligned
- Fruit is evident

And when they release them, they don't disconnect — they remain a covering, a voice, and a source of wisdom. Apostolic fathering builds generational momentum — each generation going farther, faster, and deeper because of the foundation laid before them.

Reflection Questions:

1. Am I walking as a spiritual son or living with an orphan mindset?
2. Do I have apostolic covering that provides protection, correction, and encouragement?
3. If I'm a leader, am I raising sons — or just building a brand?
4. Do I value covenant relationships, or only convenient ones?

Activation Prayer:

Father, thank You for being the perfect Father who never leaves or forsakes me. I repent for every place I've rejected spiritual authority or walked in independence and fear. Heal the orphan places in me, and teach me how to walk in sonship. If I am called to raise sons and daughters, give me wisdom, patience, and a father's heart. Help me to cover others in love, walk with them in grace, and release them in due time. Let my life and leadership reflect Your heart as a Father. In Jesus' name, amen.

7

GUARDING DOCTRINE AND CONFRONTING ERROR

O ne of the most overlooked but essential responsibilities of an apostle is to guard sound doctrine and confront error within the Church. While the modern Church often elevates charisma over content, and platform over purity, apostolic leaders are called to protect the foundations of faith and preserve the integrity of the gospel.

Paul's ministry was marked not only by miracles and mission but also by a ferocious commitment to truth. He warned the Galatians against drifting from grace, rebuked the Corinthians for tolerating sin and division, and trained Timothy and Titus to confront false teachers. Apostolic ministry is not just about building new things — it's about protecting what has been built from decay and distortion.

"Guard the good deposit that was entrusted to you—guard it with the help of the Holy Spirit who lives in us." (2 Timothy 1:14 NIV)

True apostles function like gatekeepers — not to exclude hungry people, but to protect sacred truths from compromise, corruption, and counterfeit. Without this function, the Church becomes vulnerable to deception, instability, and eventual collapse.

Apostles Are Stewards of Kingdom Truth

The apostolic calling includes stewarding doctrine, not just spiritual gifts. While prophets may bring timely words and evangelists call people into salvation, apostles ensure that the message and foundation of the faith remain intact. Apostles:

- Teach what aligns with Christ and His Kingdom
- Correct false teaching and expose heresies
- Establish clear doctrine in new churches and movements
- Train leaders to handle the Word accurately

They understand that what a generation teaches becomes what the next generation assumes, and what the third generation often forgets. Apostles labor to keep first things first — Christ crucified, risen, and enthroned; the authority of Scripture; the necessity of holiness; and the full gospel of the Kingdom.

The Danger of Doctrinal Drift

The Church doesn't usually abandon truth overnight — it drifts. This drift can happen subtly:

- When grace is preached without truth, leading to lawlessness
- When truth is preached without grace, leading to legalism

- When culture reshapes theology instead of the other way around
- When experiences are elevated above Scripture
- When unity is pursued at the cost of clarity

Apostles are called to see the drift early and speak up boldly. They do not remain silent when foundations are shifting. They understand that a compromised gospel produces compromised believers, and that error tolerated today becomes bondage tomorrow.

Confronting False Teaching with Courage and Clarity

In Galatians 1, Paul confronted a church that had been influenced by a distorted gospel. He wrote:

"Even if we or an angel from heaven should preach a gospel other than the one we preached to you, let him be under God's curse!"
(Galatians 1:8) NIV

This is apostolic clarity. Apostles love people too much to let them stay deceived. They are not afraid to name error, call for repentance, and bring correction — not to shame, but to save. Confronting false doctrine includes:

- Naming ideologies that oppose Christ (e.g., universalism, hyper-grace, works-based salvation)
- Addressing false prophecies, manipulative leadership, or unbiblical practices
- Teaching the full counsel of God, not just convenient truth
- Training leaders to rightly divide the Word and spot error

Apostolic leaders must resist the temptation to be popular and instead be faithful — faithful to the Word, to Christ, and to the people they are called to protect.

Apostles Defend the Faith Without Becoming Divisive

Apostles must walk in wisdom — able to defend the faith without becoming contentious or critical. Their confrontation is not driven by insecurity or competition but by love for the truth and for people. Their goal is not to win arguments but to win back hearts to truth. Paul told Timothy:

> *"The Lord's servant must not be quarrelsome but must be kind to everyone, able to teach, not resentful. Opponents must be gently instructed..." (2 Timothy 2:24–25 NIV)*

Apostles confront with:

- Clarity — not confusion or vague warnings
- Humility — knowing they too have been rescued by grace
- Authority — speaking from Scripture, not just emotion
- Discernment — knowing when to speak and when to stay silent

Confrontation, when done in the Spirit, leads to conviction and repentance, not division or destruction.

Apostles Preserve Apostolic Doctrine

Acts 2:42 tells us that the early Church devoted themselves to the apostles' teaching. That teaching was not just inspirational — it was foundational. It included the teachings of

Christ, the message of the Kingdom, and the instructions for holy living and spiritual maturity.

Modern apostles must preserve and pass on apostolic doctrine, ensuring that what they plant is pure, transferable, and aligned with Scripture. This means:

- Teaching the Word consistently and systematically
- Writing and documenting foundational truth
- Creating discipleship systems that reinforce doctrine
- Ensuring that leaders within their oversight are aligned and equipped

This is not rigid religiosity — it's guarding the faith once delivered to the saints (Jude 1:3).

Discerning Between Error and Immaturity

Not every mistake is heresy. Apostles must discern between error that comes from deception and error that comes from immaturity. Many young leaders or new believers may say things that are off, not because they are false teachers, but because they are still learning. True apostles:

- Correct gently
- Teach patiently
- Walk with people through their growth
- Encourage hungry hearts, even when theology needs adjustment

Apostolic correction isn't just about being right — it's about helping people become rooted and grounded in truth.

Apostles as Defenders of the Gospel in a Compromised World

We live in a time where truth is treated as optional. The pressure to conform, compromise, or stay silent is intense — especially on issues like sexuality, gender, sin, hell, and the exclusivity of Christ. Apostles must be unapologetically loyal to the gospel in a world that wants to dilute it. This means:

- Preaching repentance, not just relevance
- Holding fast to Scripture, even when it's unpopular
- Refusing to adapt the gospel to culture
- Protecting the Church from false unity that sacrifices truth

Apostles do not police the Church with pride, but guard it with tears — knowing what's at stake is not opinions, but souls.

Reflection Questions:

1. Am I growing in my understanding of sound doctrine, or drifting into opinions?
2. Do I have apostolic voices in my life who help guard me from error?
3. Am I willing to confront false teaching when I see it — with love and truth?
4. What areas of compromise have I tolerated under the disguise of tolerance?

Activation Prayer:

Father, I thank You for Your Word — living, active, and unchanging. I ask that You would give me a deep love for truth and a discerning heart. Help me recognize error, confront deception, and walk in the full counsel of Your Word. If I've compromised truth in any area, bring conviction and realignment. Let me be one who guards the deposit You've entrusted and speaks truth in love — no matter the cost. In Jesus' name, amen.

8

OPERATING IN POWER
AND PROPHETIC WISDOM

The apostolic is not merely governmental or structural—it is spiritual and supernatural. Apostles are not just architects of systems; they are carriers of heavenly authority and divine power. Wherever true apostles are sent, there should be evidence that the Kingdom of God has come—not only through alignment and order, but through miracles, deliverance, prophetic direction, and breakthrough. The apostle Paul summarized it this way:

"The signs of a true apostle were performed among you with utmost patience, with signs and wonders and mighty works." (2 Corinthians 12:12 ESV)

Apostles carry both power and prophetic wisdom. They operate in the authority of Christ to shift spiritual climates, release healing, confront darkness, and prophetically discern the strategies of God. Their ministry is not built only on teaching—it is demonstrated in the manifestation of the Spirit's power (1 Corinthians 2:4). True apostolic leadership brings both revelation and demonstration, clarity and authority, strategy and supernatural breakthrough.

Apostolic Ministry Is Marked by Power

The early Church understood apostles as those who carried Kingdom power. In Acts, when the apostles preached, people were healed. When they laid hands, people received the Holy Spirit. When they confronted darkness, demons were cast out and entire regions shifted. This power wasn't for show. It was a sign of divine backing—God confirming that His Kingdom had come near. Apostles do not just talk about power; they walk in it. They are ambassadors of the superior realm, sent to enforce Christ's victory over sin, sickness, death, and the devil. This includes:

- Healing the sick
- Casting out demons
- Working miracles and signs
- Breaking curses and cycles over territories
- Releasing divine acceleration in moments of obedience

A powerless apostolic ministry is an oxymoron. Apostles are graced to invade darkness with light and disrupt stagnation with the supernatural.

Power That Flows from Intimacy and Identity

Apostles don't manufacture power—they carry it through intimacy with Christ and alignment with Heaven. Jesus didn't just give His apostles tasks; He gave them authority (Matthew 10:1). That authority was born out of their proximity to Him. Power is not just a result of gifting—it flows from:

- Intimacy with the Father
- Obedience to God's instructions
- Walking in personal holiness
- Living in alignment with apostolic grace

The enemy recognizes spiritual authority—not titles. Apostles who walk in power know who they are in Christ, have been tested through trials, and carry a clean mantle that cannot be bought, mimicked, or faked.

Signs and Wonders That Point to the King

The goal of supernatural demonstration is not to elevate a person but to reveal a King. True apostolic miracles point people to Jesus, not to the apostle. They confirm the message of the gospel and awaken people to the reality of the Kingdom. In Acts 5:12–16, the apostles performed many signs and wonders among the people, and multitudes were added to the Lord. In Acts 13, when Elymas tried to resist Paul's message, Paul struck him with temporary blindness, and the proconsul believed because he saw the power of God.

Power without character is dangerous. But power accompanied by prophetic wisdom and humility becomes a signpost for salvation, deliverance, and transformation.

Prophetic Insight to Govern and Guide

Apostles are also marked by prophetic insight. Though not all apostles are prophets, every apostle must be prophetic—able to hear the voice of God and apply Heaven's wisdom to earthly situations. This prophetic wisdom allows apostles to:

- Discern the timing of God for assignments and transitions
- Expose demonic strategies before they unfold
- Give specific direction to leaders and churches
- Speak into cities, systems, and structures with divine solutions
- Recognize when to wait, when to war, and when to advance

Paul received prophetic dreams, angelic instructions, and directional words that shifted his movements. In Acts 27, he prophetically warned the ship's crew of the coming storm. In Acts 16, he was forbidden by the Spirit to enter Asia at that time. Apostles govern with strategic clarity because they listen deeply.

Apostles Break Open Regions with Power

Apostolic power isn't limited to healing bodies—it heals lands, families, and systems. When apostles are sent into a new region, they carry the anointing to:

- Break witchcraft and territorial bondage
- Shift spiritual climates from oppression to open heaven
- Expose hidden sin or strongholds that have hindered revival
- Call dormant churches or cities into divine awakening

This is why Paul said his aim was not to build on someone else's foundation (Romans 15:20). He was a ground-breaker, called to go where others could not go and do what others could not do. He didn't just plant churches—he established

Kingdom government through power and prophetic activation.

Balancing Revelation and Demonstration

Apostles must walk in balance. There is a danger in being overly focused on supernatural experiences while neglecting foundation and formation. But there's also danger in building structure without power. True apostles must marry revelation and demonstration—deep biblical grounding with bold supernatural expression. Apostolic ministry includes:

- Teaching truth that transforms
- Prophesying strategies from Heaven
- Healing the sick and setting captives free
- Calling people into maturity through correction and grace
- Creating cultures that expect and host the supernatural

When people encounter apostles, they should experience the wisdom of God and the power of God. Both are needed to fulfill Heaven's assignment.

Raising Teams That Walk in Power and Wisdom

Apostles don't keep the power to themselves—they equip others to walk in it. They disciple leaders and teams to:

- Prophesy with accuracy
- Heal with compassion and authority
- Cast out demons with discernment and confidence
- Hear from Heaven and lead with precision
- Partner with the Spirit, not just programs

Paul didn't just demonstrate power—he taught Timothy, Titus, and others how to walk in it. Apostolic teams carry the same power and prophetic sensitivity that rests on the apostle, creating a corporate anointing that multiplies the miraculous and sustains supernatural culture.

Reflection Questions:

1. Am I walking in both power and prophetic wisdom, or leaning too heavily on one?
2. Do I make space for God's power to move, or rely mostly on strategy and teaching?
3. Am I cultivating intimacy with God that produces authority, or just chasing manifestations?
4. Do I equip others to walk in power and discernment, or do I do it all myself?

Activation Prayer:

Father, I thank You that Your Kingdom is not in word only, but in power. I ask that You would fill me with supernatural boldness and prophetic clarity. Let me be a vessel of healing, breakthrough, and transformation. Help me to hear Your voice and respond with faith. Let signs and wonders follow my obedience, and let my life point to Jesus in all things. I receive fresh fire to walk in power and wisdom — not for my glory, but for the advancement of Your Kingdom. In Jesus' name, amen.

9

CREATING KINGDOM SYSTEMS THAT MULTIPLY

Apostles are not just visionaries; they are architects of movement. They don't simply plant churches or launch ministries—they create systems, structures, and strategies that multiply Kingdom life long after they've left the room. While some leaders focus on what they can build, apostles focus on what can reproduce. Their eyes are on generational legacy, not just short-term momentum.

In Acts, we don't just see apostles doing ministry—we see them building patterns: discipleship models, leadership structures, church planting strategies, and financial systems that allowed the gospel to multiply rapidly. Paul didn't just preach—he appointed elders, wrote governing letters, trained teams, and taught others how to replicate what he carried. Apostolic ministry is always unto multiplication.

"What you have heard from me in the presence of many witnesses entrust to faithful men who will be able to teach others also." (2 Timothy 2:2 ESV)

This is apostolic thinking: build it in such a way that it multiplies without you. Apostles don't build monuments—they establish movements that can grow, adapt, and spread the culture of the Kingdom in every sphere of society.

From Moment to Movement

One of the most important shifts in apostolic thinking is the move from moments to systems. A moment of breakthrough is powerful—but a moment not captured in a system of discipleship or development will fade. Apostles steward the move of God by creating wineskins that preserve and multiply the wine. This means apostles are always asking:

- What kind of structure will help this fruit remain?
- How can we reproduce this breakthrough in other places?
- What system ensures that sons and daughters are equipped, not just inspired?
- What's the long-term sustainability plan for this outpouring?

Without systems, revival becomes a memory. With apostolic systems, revival becomes a movement.

Apostolic Systems Are Built on Kingdom Culture

Apostles don't copy corporate models—they design systems from Kingdom DNA. These systems are not cold bureaucracies or micromanaging machines. Instead, they are relational, biblical, reproducible frameworks that reflect the values of Heaven. Apostolic systems are built on:

- Honor and humility

- Discipleship, not dependency
- Servant leadership, not celebrity culture
- Empowerment, not control
- Family and covenant, not hierarchy alone

When the system reflects the culture of the Kingdom, it becomes a life-giving structure that multiplies health, not dysfunction.

Multiplying Discipleship, Not Just Decisions

Apostles understand that decisions don't change the world—disciples do. Jesus didn't just call for converts; He made disciples who would carry His mission and model. Apostles, likewise, build discipleship systems that move people from salvation to maturity to mission. This includes:

- Clear pathways for growth and development
- Structures for accountability and pastoral care
- Training environments for spiritual gifts and leadership
- Opportunities for reproduction and multiplication

Apostolic discipleship systems equip every believer to become a leader, not just a listener. They reproduce the life of Christ in others through relational investment, biblical instruction, and Holy Spirit empowerment.

Building Financial and Organizational Systems for Expansion

Multiplication doesn't happen without financial infrastructure. Apostles create economic models that sustain ministry, fund expansion, and release Kingdom resources for Kingdom assignments. This may include:

- Teaching biblical stewardship and generosity
- Raising marketplace leaders to fund vision
- Creating income streams that fuel missions and church planting
- Structuring budgets that reflect vision and values

Apostles also establish organizational clarity: defining roles, teams, authority lines, communication systems, and operational rhythms that allow for scalability without compromise. In Acts 6, when the distribution to widows became disordered, the apostles didn't ignore it. They built a system: appointed deacons, delegated responsibility, and preserved their apostolic focus. That system released growth.

Creating Leadership Pipelines and Succession Plans

Apostolic leaders don't just fill roles—they develop people. They are constantly training, mentoring, and raising others to step into greater levels of influence and authority. They think in terms of pipelines, not positions. Apostles:

- Identify emerging leaders early
- Create spaces for growth and development
- Release responsibility incrementally
- Teach leaders how to disciple others
- Prepare the next generation to take the reins

They also plan for succession. Paul raised Timothy and Titus. Moses passed his mantle to Joshua. True apostles don't cling to power—they multiply it through sons and daughters who can run farther and faster in the future.

Reproducing Healthy Churches and Apostolic Hubs

Apostles are movement architects who plant churches, but not just for expansion—they reproduce churches that carry the same DNA, values, and structure. These churches become apostolic hubs that train, send, and multiply. Apostolic hubs:

- Are presence-centered, not program-driven
- Have fivefold leadership, not just a senior pastor model
- Prioritize discipleship and leadership development
- Function in both spiritual authority and relational accountability
- Serve as regional centers for training, deliverance, and Kingdom impact

The apostle ensures that each new work is not just functional, but foundationally sound—carrying the culture of the Kingdom and reproducing it faithfully in every location.

Systems That Serve, Not Control

One of the greatest apostolic tensions is to build systems that serve the move of God without stifling it. Systems should support vision, not suffocate it. Apostles must continually evaluate:

- Is this system still producing fruit?
- Is it adaptable to new seasons and assignments?
- Is it people-centered or process-centered?
- Is it flexible enough for the Spirit to move, yet strong enough to provide alignment?

Apostolic systems are like trellises in a vineyard. They don't produce fruit—but they support growth. When the structure gets more attention than the vine, something is wrong. But when the trellis is strong and rightly aligned, the fruit multiplies.

The Apostolic Mandate: Multiply and Mobilize

Apostles carry a Genesis 1:28 mandate:

"Be fruitful, multiply, fill the earth, and subdue it." NKJV

This is not just biological—it's spiritual. Apostles multiply:

- Leaders
- Churches
- Kingdom influence
- Financial capacity
- Regional authority
- Disciples who make disciples

They mobilize the saints for mission, equip them for the work, and create systems that scale the move of God without losing the fire of intimacy or the weight of holiness. The result is not just growth — it's Kingdom movement that transforms cities and nations.

Reflection Questions:

1. Am I thinking in terms of multiplication or maintenance?
2. What systems in my life or ministry need to be built, rebuilt, or removed?
3. Is what I'm building scalable, sustainable, and saturated in Kingdom culture?
4. Am I equipping people to reproduce or just to serve my vision?

Activation Prayer:

Father, I thank You for the wisdom and grace to build systems that multiply Your Kingdom. I surrender every man-made structure and ask for divine blueprints. Teach me to create wineskins that preserve and multiply the wine of Your Spirit. Help me raise leaders, plant works, and develop disciples who multiply the culture of Heaven. Let what I build serve the move of God, not replace it. In Jesus' name, amen.

10

BUILDING UNITY IN
THE BODY OF CHRIST

Apostles are not only builders and senders—they are also unifiers. One of the most essential, and often over-looked, functions of apostolic ministry is to build unity in the Body of Christ. Not superficial agreement, but deep spiritual alignment that reflects the oneness of Heaven. Apostles under-stand that the advancement of the Kingdom is hindered when the Church is divided, and accelerated when the Church is aligned. Jesus prayed this before going to the cross:

"That they all may be one, just as You, Father, are in Me, and I in You... so that the world may believe that You have sent Me." (John 17:21 NKJV)

True apostles carry this cry. They labor not just to plant churches or build systems, but to heal breaches, restore broken relationships, and bring diverse parts of the Body into func-tional unity. They are not empire builders or brand protectors — they are Kingdom connectors, reconcilers of movements, and fathers who contend for covenant in the Church.

Unity Is a Kingdom Imperative, Not a Human Option

Unity is not a suggestion. It is a mandate. Psalm 133 tells us that God commands a blessing where there is unity — not where there is perfection or agreement in all things, but where there is alignment in spirit and heart. Apostles understand:

- Unity is not uniformity.
- Agreement doesn't require sameness.
- Love must be stronger than difference.
- The Church cannot advance in fullness while it remains fractured.

Where pastors may focus on unity within a local church, apostles often carry a burden for unity across churches, regions, and even nations. They see the bigger picture. They think across networks. They recognize that no single church or stream carries the full picture of Christ, and that we need each other.

Apostles Heal Breaches in the Body

Apostolic grace includes the ability to repair breaches — relational, doctrinal, generational, and cultural. In Isaiah 58:12, God speaks of those who will be called "Repairer of the Breach." Apostles walk in this spirit. They are anointed to:

- Reconcile estranged leaders
- Bridge denominations and movements
- Heal wounds caused by betrayal, offense, or misunderstanding
- Bring humility where pride has divided

Apostles often become mediators in tense seasons, using

both prophetic insight and spiritual authority to bring clarity, repentance, and restoration. They don't take sides — they take responsibility for the unity of the Body and carry a Father's heart to restore it.

Apostles Break the Spirit of Competition

One of the greatest enemies of unity is competition. The orphan spirit compares, competes, and divides — but the spirit of sonship honors, collaborates, and multiplies. Apostles confront this spirit head-on. They refuse to partner with jealousy, rivalry, or empire thinking. Apostles labor to build a culture where:

- Leaders celebrate one another's fruit.
- Churches bless, not sabotage, each other.
- Movements work together for Kingdom transformation.
- Sons and daughters are secure in their place and grace.

When apostles father well, competition dies. People are not trying to prove themselves — they are trying to serve the greater purpose. Unity thrives where identity is secure.

Unity Must Be Built on Truth, Not Just Tolerance

Apostolic unity is not built on compromise—it's built on truth and honor. Unity that tolerates heresy or enables dysfunction is not biblical unity. Apostles are not afraid to confront for the sake of reconciliation, or to separate for the sake of purity when necessary.

Paul wrote to the Corinthians to address factions. He challenged Peter publicly when the gospel was compromised. Yet, he also pleaded for oneness in spirit, vision, and mission. Apostles walk the tension: they guard truth while pursuing unity. They don't unify at the expense of the gospel—but they do pursue reconciliation at any cost short of it. Apostolic unity is marked by:

- Shared foundations (Christ, the cross, the Kingdom)
- Mutual honor and recognition
- Humility to learn from one another
- Agreement in essentials, liberty in non-essentials, and love in all things

Connecting Movements, Churches, and Leaders

Apostles don't just build within their own house — they build bridges between houses. They host gatherings, lead networks, and initiate collaborations that bring different expressions of the Church together for Kingdom purpose. This may look like:

- Regional coalitions of churches contending for revival
- Apostolic networks uniting fivefold leaders under shared vision
- Marketplace and ministry collaborations for city transformation
- Mentoring relationships between generations of leaders

Where the world builds silos, apostles build bridges. Where the enemy tries to divide through offense or misunderstanding, apostles lean in and bring restoration. They understand the assignment: the Church must become one Body, in one Spirit, under one Lord.

Apostles Champion the Fivefold and Value Every Part

Apostolic unity starts with honoring the full fivefold ministry. Apostles recognize that they are not above the other gifts—they function with them. A church built on the apostolic alone is incomplete. Apostles build teams, not towers. They champion:

- Prophets who see what's coming
- Evangelists who win the lost
- Pastors who care for the flock
- Teachers who ground the house in truth

When all five graces are honored, the Church becomes healthy and whole. Apostles refuse to exalt one gift at the expense of others. Instead, they bring alignment, coordination, and honor to the diversity of Christ's Body.

Cultivating Unity Within Apostolic Houses

Before apostles unify the global Church, they must cultivate unity in their own house. Apostolic houses should be models of:

- Honor between leaders
- Submission without suppression
- Covenant relationships among team members
- Open communication and conflict resolution
- Shared wins and mutual celebration

Sons and daughters in an apostolic house are taught to

protect the culture of unity—not through blind loyalty, but through shared values and relational depth. Gossip, division, and dishonor are swiftly addressed—not in fear, but in love. Unity is not automatic. It is fought for, taught, and stewarded daily.

Unity Is Apostolic Warfare

Apostles understand that unity is spiritual warfare. Psalm 133 says God commands His blessing where unity exists. That's why the enemy attacks unity with such fury—he knows a united Church is an unstoppable Church. Apostles war for unity by:

- Praying over relationships, teams, and cities
- Teaching against offense, pride, and isolation
- Confronting divisive spirits and demonic assignments
- Hosting gatherings that call the Church into oneness

Unity is not just sentimental—it is strategic. It releases oil, blessing, and breakthrough that division never can. Apostles guard it like a gate.

Reflection Questions:

1. Am I committed to building unity, or just protecting my own corner of the Church?
2. Do I carry a heart to reconcile, restore, and bridge, or do I isolate and compete?
3. What relationships or networks has God called me to help unify?
4. How can I cultivate deeper unity in my team, house, or movement?

Activation Prayer:

Father, I thank You that You are One, and that Your Son prayed that we would be one as You are. Forgive me for every way I've contributed to division, pride, or competition in Your Body. I receive grace to become a builder of unity. Make me a reconciler, a connector, and a peacemaker. Teach me to honor every part of Your Body, to bridge movements and generations, and to guard covenant relationships. Let the unity I build release oil, blessing, and revival. In Jesus' name, amen.

11

THE COST AND CHARACTER OF APOSTLES

While the apostolic mantle is often associated with power, revelation, and governmental authority, those who walk in true apostolic grace know that it comes with a deep and personal cost. Apostles are not merely strategic leaders or dynamic pioneers—they are sacrificial servants whose lives are marked by humility, perseverance, and deep obedience to the call of God. Paul, arguably the most influential apostle in Scripture, didn't boast about his credentials first. He testified of his scars. He said:

"I bear on my body the marks of Jesus." (Galatians 6:17 ESV)

"We are hard pressed on every side, yet not crushed; we are perplexed, but not in despair; persecuted, but not forsaken; struck down, but not destroyed." (2 Corinthians 4:8–9 NKJV)

Before the apostle carries a crown, he carries a cross. Before he builds systems, he becomes one. Apostles don't just lead—they bleed. The weight of the office is not measured in how many follow them, but in how much they are willing to suffer, serve, and be conformed to Christ for the sake of others.

The Call Costs Everything

Apostolic ministry requires complete surrender. The apostle lays down personal ambition, comfort, entitlement, and even reputation. Like Paul, apostles echo the cry:

"I consider everything a loss because of the surpassing worth of knowing Christ Jesus my Lord, for whose sake I have lost all things."
(Philippians 3:8 NIV)

This loss isn't theoretical—it's tangible:

- Loss of financial security
- Loss of public approval
- Loss of stability and routine
- Loss of personal dreams that don't align with the assignment

But in every place of surrender, God deposits something eternal. Apostles are called to be living sacrifices—and from that altar, the fire of Heaven falls.

Formed in the Fire

Apostles are not formed on stages—they are formed in secret places, in storms, and in seasons of breaking. Before Paul led churches, he spent years in obscurity. Before Moses led Israel, he spent forty years in the wilderness. Before Joseph governed Egypt, he was falsely accused, imprisoned, and forgotten. The call costs because it forms character. Apostles must be:

- Crushed to carry compassion
- Humbled to carry honor
- Tested to carry truth
- Refined to carry revelation

This formation cannot be bypassed. Without it, the weight of apostolic authority will crush the unprepared. With it, the apostle becomes not just a leader—but a vessel of the Lord's heart.

The Inner Life of an Apostle

The power of apostolic ministry flows not from gifting, but from depth of character and personal holiness. The inner life of an apostle is where the foundation is laid:

- Intimacy with the Father
- Integrity in private
- Emotional maturity
- Deep submission to the Spirit
- Devotion to the Word

Apostles who do not tend to their inner life risk becoming gifted but dangerous. They may build externally, but collapse internally. True apostles maintain purity of motive, clarity of call, and consistency of heart even when no one is watching.

Living Free from the Fear of Man

One of the greatest tests of apostolic character is the fear of man. Apostles are often called to say what others won't say, go where others won't go, and do what others won't do. This means rejection is part of the journey. Apostles must be:

- Free from the need for approval
- Unmoved by applause or attack
- Anchored in identity as sons, not leaders
- Courageous in the face of opposition

Paul said, "Am I now trying to win the approval of human beings, or of God?" (Galatians 1:10). Apostles live for an audience of One. Their decisions are not driven by what is politically convenient or culturally acceptable—but by what the King requires.

Walking in Humility and Honor

Apostolic leadership is not license for pride. In fact, the higher the authority, the deeper the humility required. Apostles are not CEOs—they are servant-leaders and spiritual fathers. They carry weight without demanding honor, and lead without lording over others. True apostles:

- Give away credit rather than hoarding it
- Lift others up rather than competing
- Remain teachable, even after great success
- Submit to spiritual covering and mutual accountability

Honor flows from them because honor lives in them. They don't need titles to serve or recognition to lead. Their authority is rooted in humility and credibility, not image or platform.

Stewarding Authority with Integrity

Apostles carry authority that can build or destroy. Paul said:

"The authority the Lord gave me is for building you up, not for tearing you down" (2 Corinthians 10:8 NIV)

This means apostles must steward:

- How they use correction
- How they handle finances
- How they treat people under their leadership
- How they manage conflict and misunderstanding

Abuse of authority discredits the mantle. But when authority is stewarded with integrity, it brings life, alignment, and growth. Apostles must walk in fear of the Lord, knowing they are entrusted with souls, systems, and spheres.

Embracing the Loneliness of the Call

Apostles often walk alone—not because they're proud, but because they're called to places others have not gone. There is loneliness in pioneering, in confronting error, in building from scratch. Not everyone understands the apostolic burden. But in the loneliness, God reveals:

- Deep intimacy with Christ
- Angelic support and divine encounters
- Unexpected covenant relationships
- The fellowship of His sufferings (Philippians 3:10)

Apostles learn to find comfort in His presence, not people's praise. They know that obedience sometimes feels like isolation, but Heaven is watching—and reward is guaranteed.

Apostolic Character Produces Apostolic Legacy

At the end of the day, apostolic success is not measured by buildings, crowds, or conferences. It is measured by fruit that remains—sons and daughters walking in holiness, cities being transformed, systems reformed, and movements carrying the DNA of Christ. That kind of legacy only comes through tested character, proven faithfulness, and costly obedience. Titles fade. Platforms change. But character leaves a mark that outlives the leader.

Paul didn't just plant churches—he wrote, suffered, wept, bled, and died for the gospel. He finished his race, not with fanfare, but with faith. This is the apostolic call: to live low, love deep, and lead with fire until the end.

Reflection Questions:

1. Am I willing to pay the personal cost of apostolic leadership?
2. Is my private life consistent with my public calling?
3. Do I lead with humility and honor, or with entitlement and ego?
4. Where is the Holy Spirit forming my character through trial or transition?

Activation Prayer:

Father, I thank You for the privilege of being called to serve Your Kingdom. I surrender to the process of formation. Strip me of pride, performance, and pretense. Build in me a character that can carry Your authority without compromise. Teach me to walk humbly, lead righteously, and serve faithfully—even when it costs everything. May my life be marked by the cross, and may my leadership leave a legacy of love, holiness, and truth. In Jesus' name, amen.

12

APOSTOLIC CENTERS AND
THE FUTURE OF THE CHURCH

A s God restores apostolic leadership to the Body of Christ, He is also re-establishing apostolic centers—strategic spiritual hubs that equip, activate, and send believers into every sphere of life and culture. These centers are not defined by size or style, but by purpose, presence, and power. They are built around the government of Heaven, the presence of God, and the mission of the Kingdom.

In contrast to traditional churches that often focus on weekly services and internal care, apostolic centers are missional in nature, governmental in structure, and reformational in impact. They serve as Kingdom ecosystems that raise up mature sons and daughters, develop fivefold teams, and transform regions and spheres of influence.

As we look to the future of the Church, we must understand: God is shifting us from maintenance to mission, from gatherings to governing, from buildings to blueprints. Apostolic centers are not the next church growth fad — they are Heaven's design for a mature and mobilized Bride.

What Is an Apostolic Center?

An apostolic center is a regional or global hub of Kingdom life, led by apostolic leadership, marked by fivefold ministry, and focused on equipping, sending, and transforming. It is both a family and a base—a place where the presence of God dwells and from which people are deployed. Key features of apostolic centers include:

- Apostolic and prophetic governance
- Presence-centered worship and intercession
- Fivefold leadership functioning in unity
- Ongoing training and equipping of the saints
- Regional spiritual authority
- Systems for multiplication and cultural influence
- Deliverance, healing, and transformation culture

Apostolic centers are governmental outposts of the Kingdom, not just gathering spaces for believers. They are ecclesias —ruling assemblies that legislate Heaven's will into the earth.

Apostolic Centers vs. Traditional Church Models

While every church has value and purpose, not every church functions apostolically. Many traditional churches are centered on:

- Weekly services rather than lifestyle discipleship
- Pastoral care more than apostolic activation
- Internal programs rather than external impact
- Attendance metrics rather than equipping and sending metrics

Apostolic centers shift this focus by prioritizing:

- Equipping over entertaining
- Sending over seating
- Transformation over tradition
- Legacy over events

This doesn't mean abandoning Sunday gatherings—but it does mean redefining why we gather and what we gather around. Apostolic centers are built around Jesus as King, the Word as final authority, and the Spirit as active leader.

Characteristics of Apostolic Centers

1. Presence-Driven Culture: Apostolic centers prioritize hosting the manifest presence of God above performance, preference, or programs. Worship, prayer, fasting, and ministering to the Lord are not side ministries—they are central.
2. Fivefold Ministry Operating in Alignment: These centers are led by a team of fivefold leaders— apostles, prophets, evangelists, pastors, and teachers—working in honor and alignment to equip the saints for the work of ministry (Ephesians 4:11–13).
3. Governmental Authority in the Spirit: Apostolic centers carry spiritual jurisdiction over territories. They bind and loose, legislate in prayer, and shift atmospheres. They stand in the gate of their city and release decrees, strategies, and assignments from Heaven.
4. Multiplication and Sending Culture: Apostolic centers don't just gather people—they train and send them. They birth leaders, plant churches, launch businesses, and deploy reformers into education, government, arts, and more.

5. Deliverance, Healing, and Wholeness Ministry: These hubs function like Kingdom hospitals and military bases—healing the wounded and equipping the healed to rescue others. Inner healing, deliverance, and supernatural ministry are normal.

6. Training and Discipleship Infrastructure: Apostolic centers offer schools, intensives, and mentorship pathways that raise believers from infancy to maturity and send them into fruitful assignment.

Apostolic Centers Raise Sons, Not Consumers

The modern church has often catered to spiritual consumers—people looking to be fed, comforted, or inspired. Apostolic centers confront this culture and raise sons and daughters who:

- Embrace correction and discipleship
- Serve with ownership and maturity
- Multiply what they've received
- Carry the DNA of the house wherever they go

This transformation from consumer to son doesn't happen by accident. Apostolic centers build intentional pathways of formation, accountability, activation, and commissioning.

Apostolic Centers Influence Cities and Nations

In Acts 19, Paul established an apostolic base in Ephesus. After two years of teaching and training, the Scripture says:

"All the residents of Asia heard the word of the Lord." (Acts 19:10 ESV)

That's apostolic impact. The city was stirred, principalities were confronted, idol makers rioted, and the gospel spread like wildfire. Apostolic centers are not hidden—they shift economies, expose demonic systems, raise reformers, and invade culture with Kingdom solutions. These centers often influence:

- Marketplace and business innovation
- Education and worldview formation
- Media and arts expression
- Government and policy
- Family structures and generational healing

They function as Kingdom command centers, releasing blueprints, prophetic insight, and Holy Spirit strategies to cities and nations.

Building and Leading Apostolic Centers

Apostolic centers don't happen by accident. They must be intentionally planted, fathered, and governed. The apostle's role is to:

- Lay the foundation with vision, culture, and doctrine
- Establish fivefold teams who carry the house DNA
- Create healthy systems for equipping and sending
- Discern the regional assignment of the center
- Protect the purity, power, and purpose of the environment

Building an apostolic center takes time. It requires dying to popularity, resisting performance, and stewarding both depth and multiplication.

Apostolic Centers as Prototypes for the Future Church

The future Church will not be defined by Sunday attendance or social media engagement. It will be measured by:

- The maturity of its people
- The health of its culture
- The authority of its voice in the region
- The transformation it releases into society

Apostolic centers are prototypes of the New Testament Church—heavenly models expressing the fullness of Christ on earth. They don't replace local churches—they revive and realign them to function as Kingdom embassies once again. As the world grows darker, the Church must grow more governmental, more glorious, and more grounded. Apostolic centers are part of that strategy.

Reflection Questions:

1. Am I building or connected to a house that reflects apostolic values and function?
2. What role am I called to play in equipping, sending, or governing in this season?
3. Is our church or ministry aligned for multiplication, or centered around maintenance?
4. How can we grow in presence, fivefold leadership, and Kingdom impact?

Activation Prayer:

Father, I thank You for Your wisdom in restoring apostolic centers to Your Body. Give me eyes to see, ears to hear, and a heart to respond. Align me with Your blueprint for building a Church that advances, equips, and transforms. Help me walk in my role—whether to build, serve, lead, or support—with faithfulness and fire. Let apostolic centers rise in every city, shifting culture, discipling nations, and hosting Your glory. In Jesus' name, amen.

CONCLUSION
EMBRACING THE APOSTOLIC MANDATE

We are living in a divine reformation. God is not simply reviving churches—He is restoring Kingdom order, apostolic function, and spiritual government to the Body of Christ. What began in the book of Acts as a Spirit-filled, apostle-led, Kingdom-advancing Church is being reawakened in our generation. The cry of Heaven is going forth: "Who will be sent? Who will build what I am revealing?"

The call of the apostle is not about status—it is about sacrifice. It is not a title to wear but a burden to carry, a blueprint to steward, and a family to father. Apostles are not self-made leaders climbing the ranks of influence; they are sent ones, tested in fire, formed in obscurity, and released with authority to govern, build, align, and multiply the culture of Heaven on earth.

Rediscovering Apostolic Function

Throughout this book, we have explored the foundational functions of apostles:

- They govern with Kingdom authority, setting things in order and aligning the Church with Heaven's design.
- They build from revelation, laying foundations that reproduce and endure.
- They advance into new territory, breaking spiritual ground for the gospel to spread.
- They equip fivefold teams and raise sons, ensuring that legacy lives beyond them.
- They provide spiritual covering, fathering people into identity and maturity.
- They guard sound doctrine, confronting error and preserving truth.
- They operate in power and prophetic wisdom, demonstrating the superiority of Christ's Kingdom.
- They create systems that multiply, stewarding movement rather than moment.
- They build unity, bridging the gaps between churches, cultures, generations, and giftings.
- They walk in tested character, paying the personal cost required to carry the call.
- And they birth and lead apostolic centers that equip, send, and transform regions.

These functions are not theoretical. They are present-day realities for those who have ears to hear and hearts to obey.

The Time Is Now

There is an urgency in the Spirit. The Church cannot afford

to remain passive, consumer-driven, or personality-centered. We must rise into our Kingdom identity—a people governed by the voice of God, aligned under apostolic grace, and mobilized to disciple nations. Apostolic reformation is not coming—it is here. All over the world, God is raising apostolic houses, sending apostolic leaders, restoring fivefold teams, and positioning the Church not just to survive the shaking—but to lead through it. The call to apostolic function is a call to:

- Live from the authority of Heaven, not the approval of man.
- Build what God has shown, not what others are doing.
- Carry the burden of regions, not just the needs of individuals.
- Think generationally, multiply intentionally, and lead sacrificially.

This is not for the faint of heart—but it is for the faithful.

Your Response

Perhaps as you've read these pages, something has stirred within you. A recognition. A resonance. A realization that you are being called into apostolic alignment—maybe even into apostolic assignment. You may not feel qualified. You may still be in a hidden season. You may be leading quietly, fathering a few, building slowly, praying fervently, enduring opposition silently. But Heaven sees you. And if the Spirit is bearing witness in your heart, don't ignore it.

"As the Father has sent Me, I also send you." (John 20:21 NKJV)

You may not carry the title of apostle. That's not the point. The question is: Are you sent? Are you building what Heaven is revealing? Are you carrying weight that advances the Kingdom, restores order, and releases sons and daughters into their purpose? If the answer is yes—or even not yet, but you're willing—then this book has served its purpose.

Build What Heaven Has Revealed

In every generation, God raises builders. Nehemiah built the walls. Moses built the tabernacle. Paul built movements. Jesus said:

"I will build My Church."

Now He invites you to build with Him. This is your charge:

- Build not for applause, but for alignment.
- Build not to be seen, but to establish what is unseen.
- Build not by your own ideas, but by revelation from above.
- Build not to gather fans, but to raise sons.
- Build not alone, but with a team.
- Build not for today, but for generations.

And build with boldness, because Heaven is backing you. You are not alone. You are not overlooked. And you are not disqualified. If you are willing to yield to His process, honor His Word, and obey His voice—you are ready to be sent, to lead, to father, to build, to multiply.

The future of the Church is not celebrity-driven or conference-centered. It is apostolic, relational, governmental, supernatural, and missional. It is filled with sons and daughters who know who they are, whose they are, and where they are going. It is equipped, aligned, and unstoppable. This is the apostolic Church Jesus is building. This is the reformation we were born for. So go. Be sent. Build what Heaven has revealed. And never look back.

ABOUT THE AUTHOR

Tom Cornell is the Senior Leader of SOZO Church in Washington state, founder of Walk in the Light International and SOZO Network. Tom is married to his beautiful wife Katy and lives in the Puget Sound area with her and their three kids. He has been in ministry pastoring and teaching the body of Christ since 2008.

He has a passion to see the body of Christ moving from people with an orphan mindset to that of sonship; equipping the body to do the work of Jesus resulting in seeing the Kingdom of God manifested here on earth.

www.ingramcontent.com/pod-product-compliance
Lightning Source LLC
LaVergne TN
LVHW052036080426
835513LV00018B/2341